GEORGIAN
KHACHAPURI
AND
FILLED BREADS

Georgian Khachapuri and Filled Breads

Written and Photographed by
Carla Capalbo

THE
LITTLE
GEORGIAN
COLLECTION

CONTENTS

PREFACE

I published *Tasting Georgia, A Food and Wine Journey in the Caucasus* in 2017. It's a large travel book covering the history of Georgian food and wine and includes 70 recipes. It focuses on the winemakers and cooks whose stories taught me about the regional diversity of the country's gastronomy. Now I've decided to produce a collection of little books covering individual aspects of Georgian food and wine culture, of which this is the first.

Khachapuri – the cheese-filled bread – is a staple of Georgian cuisine and one of its iconic dishes. Other breads are filled with beans, meats and vegetables. They vary by region and season and make a good starting place for those wanting to cook Georgian food at home. They're not hard to make once you get the hang of the easy technique.

Whether you serve them as part of a complex feast or just eat them on their own, these breads are deliciously Georgian. This book includes the most traditional versions – from *khachapuri* to *lobiani* and *kubdari* – but I encourage you to be creative with the fillings, adding your favourite ingredients to make them more personal.

This book is dedicated to Judy MacDonald.

Opposite: Tbilisi old town

GEORGIA: A SHORT HISTORY

Georgia's history is unusually complex. This small country – it's about the size of Scotland or a quarter of Italy – has been fought over for millennia. Its natural beauty and strategic position between the Caucasus Mountains and the Black Sea, at the crossroads between Asia and Europe, have long made it desirable. Central Georgia's almost Mediterranean climate allows for many crops that can't easily be grown further north or south, including the grapes that feature in the country's delicious wines.

Georgia claims a blood line to Noah via his son Thargamos' great-grandson, Karthlos. The Georgians' name for their own country, Sakartvelo, derives from this. In ancient times the area was divided between the kingdoms of western Colchis (Kolkheti) and eastern Iberia. Georgia was first unified in the 9th century by King Bagrat III, and enjoyed a 'Golden Age' under King David the Builder and his granddaughter, Queen Tamar, two of its most iconic rulers. Medieval Georgia was again divided into rival kingdoms and principalities even as it battled Ottoman and Persian invaders.

Georgia was annexed by the Russian Empire in 1801 after seeking its help to defend against Ottoman and Persian attack. After a large-scale peasant revolt in 1905, the Marxist Social Democratic Party became the dominant political movement in Georgia. Joseph Stalin (Jugashvili), a Georgian Bolshevik, became a revolutionary leader there and went on to control the Soviet Union, with tragic consequences.

Georgia was briefly independent as a Democratic Republic between 1918-21 before the Red Army forcibly incorporated it into the Transcaucasian Socialist Federative Soviet Republic in 1922. In 1936 Georgia became the Georgian Soviet Socialist Republic until the dissolution of the Soviet Union. From 1972 to 1985 Eduard Shevardnadze held the post of First Secretary. Initially he fought corruption and helped reinstate the constitutional status of the Georgian language.

Georgia has been independent since 1991, when Zviad Gamsakhurdia was elected first President of Georgia. By 1992 Shevardnadze was again at the helm but became embroiled in separatist unrest that culminated in two regions – Abkhazia and South Ossetia (the Georgians prefer to call it Samachablo) – declaring autonomy from Georgia with Russia's backing. This effectively means that two large regions inside the country are off-limits for the Georgians, offering Russia a valuable foothold there.

In 2003 the bloodless 'Rose' Revolution forced Shevardnadze to resign. In 2004 Mikheil Saakashvili formed a new government and prevented the loss of a third region, Adjara, but the conflict with Abkhazia and South Ossetia led to the 2008 Russo-Georgian War. Saakashvili was voted out in 2012 and replaced by Giorgi Margvelashvili in 2013, when Bidzina Ivanishvili's Georgian Dream coalition took power.

Today Georgia is doing its best to remain an independent democracy. A tolerant Orthodox Christian country, it is the most pro-European nation in the region. Georgia is currently increasing its positive international profile, with food and wine tourism playing an important part in that process.

Opposite: Khertvisi fortress, Samtskhe-Javakheti

THE GEORGIAN *SUPRA*

The Georgians are wonderfully hospitable, especially when they're hosting family and guests at the table. The *supra*, or feast, holds legendary status. That's where the passion for food, wine, music and good conversation come together. In Georgia the table is never empty. When you sit down for a meal, dishes already filled with a variety of colourful foods are arranged along the table from which the diners serve themselves. As the meal progresses hot dishes arrive in waves to complement them. So an initial assortment of vegetable dishes and condiments may be joined by beans, stewed and grilled meats, dumplings and filled breads.

The Georgian way of eating – many dishes to share with friends – feels modern but has ancient roots. The art of combining foods with exciting taste combinations – from sour to sweet, spicy to aromatic – has developed over centuries as the country's occupiers added their culinary riches to Georgia's. An abundant use of fresh vegetables, nuts and herbs makes the cuisine even more vibrant. If the full *supra* of at least 10 dishes seems too much for one cook to produce, try making a lighter version of 4 or 5, with at least one kind of filled bread.

Opposite: Supra table, Lagazi Wine Cellar, Kakheti

ABOUT GEORGIAN FILLED BREADS

The ultimate comfort food, no Georgian meal would be complete without at least one kind of filled bread. They appear during a *supra* to accompany the other hot dishes but are also great as snacks or lighter meals by themselves. You can take them on picnics or reheat them for breakfast.

Khachapuri – the bread filled and sometimes also topped with cheese – is the most popular and best known. It has at least five distinct regional styles and countless variations.

Many others exist. Filled breads vary by region and by the preferences of individual families and their cooks. They can be made round or square, big or small. In this book you'll find the most delicious, with fillings ranging from beans and greens to spiced meat.

Differences may depend on the type of dough being used (yeast or other leavening agents), the cooking method (oven-baked or stove-top), the shape, filling or season… the list is endless. But in each the principle of a bread dough with a filling is the same. Once you've mastered the technique, create your own!

(You'll find a complete list of the recipes in this book on p. 5)

Opposite: Lobiani (front) and mkhlovani, Racha-Lechkhumi

ABOUT THE RECIPES

These recipes have been written for people who may never have tasted Georgian food and for those who already love it. So I've given measured ingredient suggestions throughout. This isn't really the way Georgians who are familiar with these recipes cook. They rely on experience, adding a sprinkling of spices or handful of herbs where they know they'll work.

I collected the recipes from families throughout Georgia and tested them using British and American ingredients. The results are somewhat different from the originals as basic ingredients – including flour and cheese – vary from place to place. Stick to high-quality ingredients and your dishes will always taste delicious.

Measurements are given in metric, imperial and US systems, including the US cup (240 ml / 8 fl oz) but I always weigh my dry ingredients: scales are more accurate than the cup system.
The spoons are UK/US standard:

   1 tablespoon (tbsp) = approximately 15 millilitres (ml)

   1 teaspoon (tsp) = approximately 5 ml

I usually portion each bread into 8 pieces, but you can cut them smaller to go with aperitifs or larger for main meals.

ABOUT GEORGIAN CHEESES
FOR *KHACHAPURI*

Khachapuri is a hot, flattish bread oozing with melted cheese in the centre. The kind of cheese you use determines the character of your *khachapuri*. In Georgia it's usually a lightly salted, fresh cow's milk cheese that's made at home or sold in the markets and that gives a characteristic sour tang and curd-rich texture. In some areas – including western Samegrelo – the favoured cheese is *sulguni*, a stretched-curd cheese (made like mozzarella) that gives a stringier consistency.

Outside of Georgia and other rural countries it's quite difficult to find these fresh cheeses: few of us have a cow providing us with daily milk from which to fashion our own. So to come close in taste and texture I've found it best to blend several cheeses for the filling. A mix of plain curd (or cottage) cheese, mozzarella (the kind used for pizzas as the fresh balls have to much liquid in them), farmer's cheese or cow's milk feta all work well. I sometimes even add a little cheddar or Swiss cheese to the blend to augment flavour and tang. It's up to you!

Opposite: Cheese stalls, Bodbiskhevi market, Kakheti

HOW THE GEORGIANS FORM THEIR FILLED BREADS

The idea is simple: a thin envelope of bread dough containing a flat, even centre of cheese, meat or vegetables, that is oven baked or cooked in a skillet. Every woman in Georgia makes it look easy. However getting the dough even – without visible seams or thicker parts of bread – is surprisingly tricky.

The Georgians pat or roll their rather soft dough into a disc, heap the filling on top in a substantial ball, and then draw the dough up and around the filling to enclose it completely, pinching the dough together at the seams. If there is a topknot of dough, it's sometimes removed.

The ball is then turned over – hiding the seams on the underside – patted once more into a disc shape, and rolled or patted out to make the bread thinner.

A small air hole is poked in the centre of the top, and the bread is baked, with or without an egg wash. (Alternatively, some people cook their breads in a dry skillet on the stove, without the added air hole.) Often the bread is started on a wood-burning stove or in a pan, and then finished in the oven.

I prefer the simpler, foolproof method described on pp. 27-28. It's similar to theirs in all but shape, as it produces square breads instead of round.

IMERETIAN *KHACHAPURI*

This is the most popular version of *khachapuri*, and despite originating in Imereti region, it's found throughout Georgia. This bread is filled with a mixture of cheeses and is oven-baked or cooked in a dry pan on the stove. Use this as your master recipe, following the individual recipes in the book for other fillings.

Every cook in Georgia has their own preferred method of making dough for *khachapuri* and other filled breads. They vary from slow-rising yeast doughs to doughs made more quickly that rely on acidic live yogurt (*matsoni*), baking soda (bicarbonate of soda) and even Georgian sparkling mineral water to activate the dough. The idea is to make a light, airy dough.

I'm opting for two doughs: a yeast dough as well as a dough that uses yogurt and baking soda. They're both good but they produce different textures and styles for the breads. The yeast dough is the classic and makes a better bread crust, but the yogurt dough takes an hour less time so it's useful when guests drop by unexpectedly and you want to whip up a quick *khachapuri*.

As I travelled through the regions watching home cooks producing these breads, I found that most Georgians keep their *khachapuri* doughs simple: the cheese fillings are so rich there's no need to add lots of butter or milk to the dough. They all rub the top of the baked bread with butter as soon as it comes out of the oven. This softens the bread – stopping it from cracking or becoming leathery – adds a sheen, and enriches it.

THE MASTER DOUGH RECIPE (YEAST)

It's almost as easy to make two breads as to make one, and they can be reheated if any are left over, so here are the amounts for 1 or 2 breads.

PREPARATION **120 minutes (including rising time)**
BAKE **20-25 minutes**

FOR **2** BREADS, **8** SERVINGS EACH
400 g / 14 oz strong / bread flour
1 tsp sugar
1 tsp quick-acting/instant yeast
1 tsp salt
290 ml / 10 fl oz / 1¼ cups warm water
1 tbsp sunflower oil

FOR ONE BREAD, **8** SERVINGS
225 g / 8 oz strong / bread flour
1 tsp sugar
¾ tsp quick-acting /instant yeast
¾ tsp salt
150 ml / 5 fl oz / ½ cup plus 2 tbsp warm water
1 tbsp sunflower oil

HOW TO MAKE THE DOUGH

These doughs are best made in the traditional way, by hand, mixing the warm water into the dry ingredients in a large bowl and kneading on a floured board for 4–6 minutes, until the dough is smooth. Don't over-work the dough or it will toughen.

If you prefer to use a processor: Place the flour, sugar, yeast and salt in the food processor's bowl and process briefly. Pour in the warm water and process again. The dough will come together and form a ball. Continue processing for 2 minutes. Turn the dough out onto a lightly floured surface. Dust your hands with flour and knead the dough for another 2 minutes. It should be slightly sticky and not too firm.

For both systems: Spread the oil around the bottom and sides of a large bowl. Place the dough ball in the bowl, turning it once to pick up some of the oil. Cover the bowl with a clean, dry tea cloth and place it in a warm place for 90–115 minutes. (If you're not using the oven for anything else, turn it on low for 5 minutes before you knead the dough. Then put the bowl with the dough into the turned-off oven to rise.)

When the dough has risen to about twice its original volume, punch it down, turn it out onto a lightly floured board and knead it for just a minute to form a smooth ball.

Preheat the oven to 170°C/325°F/Gas 3. Place a flat, heavy iron baking sheet on a rack in the centre of the oven. Fill and form the bread while the oven heats up.

TO FILL ONE *KHACHAPURI*

I like using a combination of four cheeses, in equal parts: For each Imeretian *khachapuri* I use 60g/2oz each of cottage cheese, crumbled cow's milk feta, grated mozzarella and grated cheddar, emmental or other Swiss cheese, but you can experiment and use your own favourites.

> **225g/8oz mixed cheeses, at room temperature**
> **freshly grated black pepper**
> **1 egg, beaten**

Mix the four cheeses in a small bowl. Season with pepper. If you like, also add half of the beaten egg, keeping the rest to paint on the top of the bread.

HOW TO FORM AND BAKE THE FILLED BREADS MY WAY

On a lightly floured surface, roll and pat the dough into a square about 30cm/12in wide. Straighten the edges by cutting away any bulges. Shape your filling evenly into another square, like a diamond in the centre of the dough square (see top photo).

One at a time, fold each corner of dough up towards the centre, pinching the seams firmly as you go to seal the bread, like making an envelope. Turn the bread carefully over onto a sheet of baking paper. Pat or roll it out gently to stretch the bread a little more. If you're going to bake the bread in the oven, make a small air hole in the centre and paint the top with a little beaten egg.

Slide a flat baking tray under the bread's baking parchment, open the oven and slide the bread – on its paper – onto the preheated baking tray already in the oven. This will ensure the underside of the bread is crisp and well cooked. Make sure the heat source for your oven is coming only from below or you will inadvertently grill your bread and toughen its dough.

Bake for 25–30 minutes, or until the top is golden and the dough is cooked. The bread may rise, but don't worry, it will settle again after baking.

Remove the bread from the oven and immediately rub a tablespoonful of butter all over the top of the bread. This keeps the dough soft and pliable. Cut into squares or wedges and serve hot.

To reheat a filled bread, sprinkle or rub a little water over the top of the bread and place it in a preheated oven at 180°C/350°F/Gas 4 for about 10 minutes, or until the filling is heated through.

THE SKILLET METHOD

If you prefer to cook the bread in a skillet on the stove, don't make the air hole or paint the top with the egg. This method works best with the yeast dough.
Use a heavy skillet or non-stick frying pan a little

bigger than the bread (if the pan is too thin, the bread will burn). Make sure your filled bread has no extra flour on it or this too will burn. Heat the pan, without oil, over medium to low heat and slide the bread into it. Cook slowly for about 10–12 minutes, checking occasionally to make sure the underside is not burning. When the dough has set on the first side and it's a light gold, turn the bread over and continue cooking 8–10 minutes more.

Slide the bread onto a plate and rub about 1 tablespoonful of butter onto the top of the dough. Serve hot.

THE MASTER DOUGH
(YOGURT AND BAKING SODA)

This dough is easy to make and seems happiest when mixed by hand (as opposed to in the processor) and baked in the oven. Make sure your yogurt is at room temperature.

FOR ONE BREAD, **8** SERVINGS
PREPARATION **60 minutes**
COOK **25-30 minutes**

170 g / 6 oz / 1½ cups strong/bread flour
½ tsp salt
¾ tsp baking soda (bicarbonate of soda)
170 g / 6 oz / ¾ cup unsweetened live yogurt, at room temperature
1 tbsp sunflower oil
flour, for kneading

In a medium mixing bowl, combine the flour with the salt and baking soda. Stir in the yogurt and half of the oil. Mix well using your hands.

Lightly flour a work surface. Turn the dough out onto it and knead the dough, adding more flour if necessary, until it's smooth and has stopped stick-ing to the surface (don't add too much flour as it should be quite a soft dough). Use the remaining oil to lightly oil a clean, medium mixing bowl. Put the dough ball into it, turning it over so the top is oiled too.

Cover the bowl with a clean tea cloth and leave it in a warm place for about 45 minutes. Then follow the instructions for forming and filling the bread (see pp. 20-21, 27-28).

Overleaf: Summer supra table, Kakheti

Megrelian *khachapuri*

MEGRULI KHACHAPURI　მეგრული ხაჭაპური

The most indulgent version of *khachapuri* comes from Samegrelo, in western Georgia. Not only does it have a filling of cheese like the Imeretian, it also has a mixture of grated cheese and egg spooned over the top of the bread just before baking. As you can see from the photos of this style of *khachapuri* on p. 1, 2, 34 and 60, the results vary in thickness and due to different oven types (yes, you can bake it in a pizza oven) but the result is always a cheese-lover's delight.

Follow the steps for Imeretian *khachapuri* in the Master Recipe pp. 22-23, filling the dough with all but 3 tablespoons of the grated cheese for each *khachapuri* you are making. Mix the reserved cheese with the remaining half egg.

When the bread has been formed, spoon or paint the top with the egg and cheese mixture. Make an air hole in the centre and bake as for the Imeretian bread until the top is golden brown.

Opposite: Khachapuri baked in a wood-burning oven, Nosiri restaurant, Samegrelo

Adjarian *khachapuri*

ADJARULI KHACHAPURI აჭარული ხაჭაპური

This open-faced cheese bread, with its bright yellow egg yolk at the centre, is the most iconic dish from the Autonomous Republic of Adjara, on the Black Sea. A favourite throughout Georgia and beyond, the diner stirs the hot cheese into the egg to finish its cooking. Its thick edges may be enriched with cheese. The diner breaks off a chunk, dipping it into the gooey filling.

Follow the Master Recipe yeast dough on p. 24. You will need one extra egg for the centre of each *khachapuri* made with 225 g / 8 oz flour, and 15 g / ½ oz / 1 tbsp soft butter for serving the bread.

After the yeast has risen, preheat the oven to 170 °C / 325 °C / Gas 3. Place a flat, heavy metal baking sheet on a rack in the centre of the oven.

Punch the dough down, turn it out onto a lightly floured surface and knead for a minute to form an even ball. Roll it into a circle 30 cm / 12 in in diameter on a piece of baking paper. Sprinkle 3 tablespoons of the grated cheese along the top and bottom edges of the dough and roll them in towards the centre to form a boat shape with pointed ends. Pinch the dough to stop it unfolding.

Fill the centre of the 'boat' with the remaining cheese mixture. Bake until the crust is golden and the cheese is bubbling, about 25 minutes. Carefully slide a raw egg into the centre of the bread and put it back into the oven for 2–3 minutes more. The yolk should still be runny.

Remove from the oven and put the butter on top of the egg. Serve immediately, stirring the egg into the hot cheese and butter.

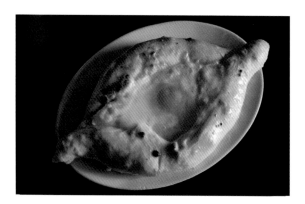

Gurian Christmas *khachapuri*

GURULI GHVEZELI   გურული ღვეზელი

This special bread is made in all Gurian houses on Christmas day and contains hard-boiled eggs in addition to the usual *khachapuri* cheese filling. It's popular throughout the Christmas and New Year season and is sometimes baked with a coin or nut inside. The person who gets the hidden treasure will have a prosperous new year.

This can be baked either as small, individual breads or as one larger bread. The bread's shape changes too, into a rounded crescent or half circle. I love the addition of the eggs as it makes a more substantial bread with an extra dimension. Perfect for lunch with a salad all year long.

Following the Master Recipe on p. 24, make the dough as described, for 1 or 2 breads. Prepare the cheeses for the filling. You'll need 2 hard-boiled eggs for every 225 g/8 oz of cheese. (You won't need to add any raw egg to the cheese.)

When the dough has risen, roll it out into a circle or oval 30 cm/12 in wide on a piece of parchment

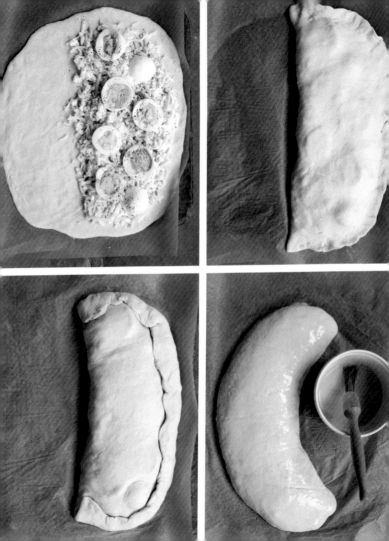

paper. Distribute the cheese evenly over half of the circle. Top with sliced egg and some ground black pepper. Cover the filling with the other half of the dough, pinching it all along the border to seal it. Fold the sealed edge in onto the bread. Using the paper to help you, turn the bread over, hiding the seams underneath. Shape the bread into a crescent, folding the pointed tips under to seal them.

Beat an egg yolk with a teaspoon of water and paint it evenly over the top of the bread. Prick a few small air holes in the dough with a fork.

Slide the bread onto the preheated heavy baking tray in the oven and bake until the top is golden, about 25–30 minutes (smaller breads will take less time). Rub the top with 1 tablespoon butter while still hot. Slice the bread into slices crosswise to serve.

Cheese and potato bread

KHABIZGINA ხაბიზგინა

This comforting and substantial bread is a popular staple in the high Caucasus mountains of Kazbegi and South Ossetia where potatoes were often the only locally grown vegetable.

Boil your potatoes with the skins on so they don't absorb too much water. Use a combination of sheep's cheese and cow's for this recipe, such as feta or pecorino and mozzarella. Use either of the dough recipes on pp. 24 or 30, and follow the bread-making method on p. 25.

SERVES **8**
PREPARATION **40 minutes plus 90 minutes rising time**
COOK **25-30 minutes**

FOR THE FILLING
260 g / 9 oz boiled potatoes, skins on
30 g / 1 oz / 2 tbsp butter, melted
200 g / 7 oz grated or crumbled cheese
½ tsp salt, or to taste
freshly ground black pepper

Peel the potatoes and grate them using a large grater into a medium mixing bowl. Fold in the butter and cheese without compacting the filling too much. Season with salt and pepper.

When the dough has almost finished rising, pre-heat the oven to 170°C/325°F/Gas 3.

When the dough has risen, punch it down and knead it quickly into a ball on a lightly floured surface. Roll it out into a 20cm/12in square and follow the instructions on pp. 26-27 for how to fill and bake the bread. Serve hot or warm.

Meskhetian *khachapuri*

MESKHURI KHACHAPURI   მესხური ხაჭაპური

The buttery, layered dough of Meskhetian, or *penovani khachapuri* speaks of the influence of the Ottoman empire in southern Georgia. Local women make the dough by skilfully stretching it as thin and wide as strudel.

You can achieve a similar result much more easily by using all-butter puff pastry. It produces an elegant pie that is delicious straight from the oven when the cheese is oozing hot and the pastry is crisp. Use a mixture of your favourite cheeses, as in the Master Recipe, p. 26. This kind of pastry also works well with the other fillings in this book for quick tasty breads.

SERVES 4-6
PREPARATION 10 minutes
COOK 30 minutes

1 roll ready-made all-butter puff pastry, chilled
75 g / 2½ oz / ⅔ cup grated or crumbled cheeses
80 g / 3 oz / ¾ cup grated pizza mozzarella
1 egg yolk

Preheat the oven to 220°C/425°F/Gas Mark 7. Place a heavy flat baking tray in the centre of the oven while the oven is preheating.

Unroll the dough and cut it into a square about 22 cm/9 in on each side. Let it sit at room temperature on a lightly floured board while you prepare the cheese. (Refrigerate the remaining dough and use it for something else).

Combine the cheeses, including the mozzarella, in a mixing bowl.

Spread the cheese in an even layer onto the dough square. Pick up two opposing corners of the dough and bring them into the centre, pinching them together to hold. Repeat with the remaining corners. The parcel will look like a closed envelope with slighly higher outer edges. Pinch the seams together so it doesn't come apart during baking. Turn the bread over onto a sheet of baking paper.

Paint the top with the beaten egg yolk. Slide the bread onto the preheated baking tray and bake for 25-30 minutes, or until the top is a deep golden brown. Cut into pieces and serve hot or warm.

Opposite: Cows grazing beneath the
Caucasus Mountains, Kakheti

Svanetian meat-filled bread

KUBDARI   კუბდარი

One of the most delicious filled breads, *kubdari* comes from the highland region of Svaneti, in the Great Caucasus mountains. It's filled with lightly spiced chunks of tender pork or beef, onions and herbs. A meal in istelf, *kubdari* also complements vegetable dishes at a *supra*.

Follow the Master Recipe for the yeast dough for 2 breads and method on p. 24.

SERVES **8-16**
PREPARATION **40 minutes**
COOK **45 minutes**

I RECIPE OF YEAST DOUGH FOR 2 BREADS

FILLING FOR TWO BREADS:
  400 g / 14 oz lean pork or beef fillet
  30 g / 1 oz / 2 tbsp butter
  75 g / 2½ oz / ½ cup finely chopped onion
  4 g / 1 garlic clove, finely chopped
  ⅛ tsp ground chilli, or more to taste
  1 tbsp tomato paste
  ½ tsp ground blue fenugreek
  ¼ tsp coriander seed, crushed
  ⅛ tsp ground cumin
  1 tsp fresh dill, minced
  ½ tsp salt
  2 tbsp minced fresh coriander/cilantro
  1 tbsp sunflower oil
  2 tbsp water
  butter

While your dough is rising, make the filling. Cut the meat into small, bite-size pieces.

Heat the butter in a small heavy saucepan and gently sauté the onion until it starts to become translucent, 6–7 minutes. Stir in the garlic and chilli and cook for 2–3 minutes more. Remove from the heat and stir in the tomato paste and dry spices. Stir the onion mixture into the meat with the remaining ingredients and mix well. Refrigerate until you're ready to use.

Place a heavy baking tray in the centre of the oven and preheat the oven to 180°C/350°F/Gas 4 at least 15 minutes before you want to bake the breads.

Divide the dough and filling in half and form the breads following the instructions on pp. 20 or 27.

Bake on the preheated baking tray for 30–35 minutes, or until the top begins to brown and the meat is cooked through. Remove from the oven and immediately spread a little butter all over the top and sides of the bread to keep it soft. Serve hot.

Opposite: Charkviani Guest House, Ushguli, Svaneti

Bread with greens

MKHLOVANI მხლოვანი

Breads stuffed with wild and farmed greens are popular in the hilly regions of Georgia. Beet greens and stems are nutritious and taste great yet they're too often thrown away. If you can't find them, substitute fresh chard and spinach, supplemented by wild foraged leaves if possible. This bread works well with both yeast and yogurt doughs (use unsweetened, live yogurt). The quantity of filling given is for one bread.

SERVES **6-8**
PREPARATION **40 minutes (plus 90 minutes salting/ dough rising)**
BAKE **20 minutes**

FOR THE FILLING
450 g / 1 lb beet greens, chard and/or spinach, with their stems
1½ tsp salt
45 g / 1½ oz / 3 tbsp butter, melted
freshly ground black pepper

Make the dough from the instructions on pp. 24 or 30. While it is rising, prepare the filling.

Pick through the greens and stems carefullly, washing them in several changes of water to remove grit. Spin or pat dry to remove excess water. Chop roughly. Sprinkle lightly with the salt and place in a colander for 1 hour.

Foraged greens at Tbilisi market in March

Rinse the greens in cold water and shake them to remove the excess liquid. Push them into a medium saucepan, over medium heat, and cover. You want to wilt the leaves so they'll be easier to work with. As soon as they have wilted, remove them from the pan to a bowl, leaving any liquid at the bottom of the pan, and toss with the butter. Season with black pepper.

Place a flat, heavy baking tray on a rack in the centre of the oven and preheat to 170°C/325°F/ Gas 3.

Follow the instructions of pp. 26-28 for filling and baking the bread.

Breads with beans

LOBIANI   ლობიანი

This is an iconic dish from the forested hills of Racha. It's most often served with a traditional filling of plain, mashed beans. Some Rachans add the fat from locally smoked hams to the beans for a distinctive smoky taste. Speck, smoked prosciutto from northern Italy, can bring similiar depth of flavour. A vegetarian version follows at the end of the recipe. If you're in a hurry, use drained and rinsed canned beans. This recipe is enough to fill one bread, starting with 175 g/ 6 oz/ 1 cup dried beans.

SERVES **6-8**
PREPARATION **30 minutes (plus 90 minutes for dough rising)**
COOK **25 minutes**

FOR THE BEAN FILLING
720 ml / 24 fl oz / 3 cups plain cooked beans (plus some cooking liquid)
60 g / 2 oz / 4 tbsp butter
6 paper-thin slices Speck, chopped
1 egg, beaten
salt

Prepare the dough for 1 bread on pp. 24 or 30. While it is rising, make the filling.

Mash or purée the beans by pushing them through a sieve or using a hand processor or crusher. The purée should be fairly stiff – like mashed potatoes – but if it seems too dry, add a few spoonfuls of the bean cooking water.

In a small, non-stick frying pan, melt the butter over medium heat. Add the beans and the optional Speck. Cook for 5 or 6 minutes, stirring frequently, until the beans are heated through. Taste for seasoning and allow to cool before filling the bread.

Place a flat, heavy baking tray in the centre of the oven. Preheat the oven to 180°C/350°F/Gas 4.

Follow the instructions on pp. 20 or 27 for filling and baking the bread, painting the top with a little beaten egg before baking. Bake for 20–25 minutes, or until the top is light gold. Rub the top of the bread with butter as soon as it's out of the oven. Serve hot.

HERBED HOT BEAN FILLING (ALTERNATIVE FILLING)

For this spicier, vegetarian filling it's nice to leave some of the beans whole for added texture, so only mash or purée about three-quarters of the beans.

FOR THE FILLING
30 g / 1 oz / 2 tbsp butter
115 g / 4 oz / ¾ cup finely chopped onion
720 ml / 24 fl oz / 3 cups cooked beans (plus a bit of cooking liquid)
8 g / ¼ oz / 2 garlic cloves, chopped
½ tsp ground blue fenugreek
½ tsp coriander seed, crushed
1 tsp salt
¼ tsp chilli flakes, or to taste
20 g / ⅔ oz / ½ cup chopped fresh coriander / cilantro
1 tbsp water

Heat the butter in a small frying pan and sauté the onion until it is translucent, 4–5 minutes. Tip the onions into a medium bowl with the garlic, herbs and spices. Use a hand blender to purée them lightly. Add three-quarters of the beans and purée again. The mixture doesn't have to be perfectly smooth. If it's too thick to purée, add a spoonful of water. Add the remaining beans to the purée and mix well using a spoon. The purée should be fairly stiff. Taste for seasoning, adding salt as necessary. Allow to cool before filling the bread.

Lobiani, Hotel Gallery, Oni, Racha

WHAT TO EAT WITH *KHACHAPURI*

Khachapuri and its fellow filled breads are wonderfully versatile. At a *supra*, they will be served halfway through the meal while the vegetables and meats are still on the table and they make the perfect complement to cucumber and tomato salads (topped with lots of fresh herbs), aubergines/eggplants dressed with lightly spiced walnut pastes, and stewed beans or meats. The breads act as an anchor to the more vibrant flavours of these dishes and also are great for mopping up the juices. They go well with ratatouille and vegetable curries too.

You can also feature them in simpler meals. I like making *khachapuri* or *kubdari* for lunch with a salad of mixed greens, or taking the Gurian version (with its added hard-boiled eggs) on a picnic along with spicy *ajika* (a Georgian condiment) or an Indian chutney. I even love eating leftover *khachapuri* for breakfast! And if you keep a roll of puff pastry in the freezer, you can whip up a *khachapuri* if friends are coming over for drinks: just cut it up into smaller pieces as finger food. I always add a handful of chopped tarragon, coriander/cilantro and basil to the cheese for a more aromatic and complex flavour. And these breads go perfectly with white, amber or red wines.

INDEX

Carla Capalbo is an award-winning food, wine and travel writer and photographer. She has written many books about Italian food and wine. Her most recent book, *Tasting Georgia: A Food and Wine Journey in the Caucasus* received rave reviews and won the *Guild of Food Writers*' Food & Travel award and the *Gourmand International* Best Food Book UK award.

Carla is based in London but spends lots of time in Georgia, Italy and beyond. She leads food and wine tours in Georgia and Italy, and writes for many premium international magazines.

www.carlacapalbo.com
www.tastinggeorgia.com

Georgian Khachapuri and Filled Breads
Text, recipes, photographs and map © Carla Capalbo 2018
Cover Mkhlovani (front) and Lobiani, Racha-Lechkhumi
p. 1 Megrelian khachapuri
p. 2 Zaira Jgharkava with her Megrelian khachapuri, Oda Family Winery, Samegrelo

First published 2018 by Pallas Athene (Publishers) Ltd,
Studio 11A, Archway Studio, 25-27 Bickerton Road, London N19 5JT
www.pallasathene.co.uk

Editing, design and layout: Carla Capalbo, Anaïs Métais, Alexander Fyjis-Walker

Printed in China

ISBN 978-1-84368-170-0